KATHY and DAVID BLACKWELL

SOLO TIME FOR VIOLIN

BOOK 2

GW00578171

Contents

With thanks to Simon Stace for reviewing the pieces in this book, Ros Stephen for recording the violin tracks, Ken Blair for producing the CD, and Laura Jones and Phil Croydon at OUP for all their help. KB & DB.

The CD includes piano-only backings (tracks 1–18) for all pieces and a selection of full performances, detailed above the relevant pieces, (tracks 19–23). CD credits: David Blackwell (piano); Ros Stephen (violin).

OXFORD
UNIVERSITY PRESS

Great Clarendon Street, Oxford OX2 6DP, England
This collection and each individual work within it © Oxford University Press 2015
Unauthorized arrangement or photocopying of this copyright material is ILLEGAL.

Kathy and David Blackwell have asserted their right under the Copyright, Designs and Patents Act, 1988, to be identified as the Authors of this Work.

Impression: 5
ISBN 978-0-19-340478-6
Music and text origination by Julia Bovee
Printed in Great Britain

1. Prelude in D

from Six Preludes for Harpsichord, BWV 936

Johann Sebastian Bach (1685–1750)

arr. KB & DB

A prelude is a short instrumental piece, often acting as an introduction to something else or paired with another piece. Bach's famous collection of preludes and fugues for keyboard, *The Well-Tempered Clavier*, uses all 24 major and minor keys, and the preludes explore a wide variety of styles. This prelude is an arrangement of the fourth of a set of six preludes for harpsichord by Bach. The dynamics are suggestions, as composers at this time generally left these for the performer to decide. The ornament at bar/measure 31 is a mordent; it should begin on the upper note and can be short or long (or it could be omitted). Play with a light detached style.

2. Pensée fugitive

track 2

Moritz Moszkowski (1854–1925)
arr. KB & DB

Andante con moto ♪ = 100

The German composer Moszkowski was famous for his talent as an outstanding pianist. He suffered badly from stage fright, however, and as a result he concentrated more on composing and conducting. This expressive piece was originally written for piano (Op. 94 No. 4), and the title means 'fleeting thought'. The wide intervals and chromaticisms found in the central section are very characteristic of music from the Romantic era.

3. Petite Fantaisie—Boléro

track 3 (Andante con moto)

Charles Dancla (1817–1907)
arr. KB & DB

The French violinist, composer, and teacher Charles Dancla wrote many educational and instructional compositions for violin. This piece was originally written for violin and piano (Op. 126 No. 5). The bolero, used as the central section of this Fantaisie, is a Spanish dance in triple time, and many composers have used this dance as an inspiration for their compositions.

Boléro

4. Rondo

track 5: piano only; track 19: violin and piano

from 12 Violin Duos, Op. 38

Jacques-Féréol Mazas (1782–1849)

arr. KB & DB

Mazas was a French composer and violinist who wrote a number of studies and duets for violin. In rondo form a main theme returns with contrasting sections in between.

This Rondo is an arrangement of the last movement of Duo No. 2, from 12 Violin Duos, Op. 38.

5.   Odessa Bulgar

Klezmer trad.
arr. KB & DB

Klezmer is the traditional music of the Jewish communities of central and eastern Europe and features dance tunes and instrumental pieces typically played at weddings and other celebrations. The Bulgar is a fast dance in 4/4 time, and this particular tune is from Odessa, a city in Ukraine on the north-western shore of the Black Sea and an important Jewish centre (as well as the birthplace of two famous classical violinists, David and Igor Oistrakh). This tune is based on the Misheberakh

mode, sometimes known as the Ukrainian Dorian scale:

Play with lots of energy to capture the lively characteristics of this dance music. Klezmer violinists traditionally use open strings rather than 4th fingers to increase the volume of their playing when accompanying dancers, and the tunes are often ornamented.

6. Cradle song

from *Lyric Pieces*, Op. 68 No. 5

Edvard Grieg (1843–1907)

arr. KB & DB

Edvard Grieg was a Norwegian composer whose music has become some of the best known and most popular of all classical music. This includes the Piano Concerto in A minor and 'Morning' and 'In the Hall of the Mountain King' from the incidental music for Henrik Ibsen's play *Peer Gynt*. Grieg drew on traditional Norwegian folk music in many of his compositions and also composed violin sonatas and many miniature pieces for piano. This piece is taken from Book 9 of his *Lyric Pieces*, a collection of 66 characterful pieces for solo piano published in ten books.

7. Sugar with Cinnamon

track 8: piano only;
track 21: violin and piano

Lavildevan
arr. KB & DB

Lavildevan was a Brazilian composer active at the end of the nineteenth century, and known only by his surname. Brazilian dance music of this time was a blend of European and Afro-Caribbean musical styles, with the regular phrases and clear harmonic structure of European dances enriched by the traditional rhythms of Latin-American dance music, here represented by the *cinquillo* (the five-note rhythm found e.g. in bar 23) and

the *habanera* (the characteristic rhythm from the Cuban dance of the same name, heard in bar 25 and throughout the piano accompaniment). This blend gives rise to the title of this piece, with 'sugar' and 'cinnamon' standing for white and black musical characteristics. Be careful to contrast the *cinquillo* and triplet rhythms when side by side. A number of bars start with a rest—be sure not to hold on the note from the previous bar.

8.   Sail to the blue

track 9

Kathy and David Blackwell

A jazz waltz is written in the characteristic 3/4 time of a waltz but adds the syncopations of jazz. Keep the syncopations light to give the impression of a graceful dance. The quavers need to be swung, so the rhythm of bar 5 is more like this:

and the rhythm of bar 47 like this:

9. Slavonic Dance

track 10: piano only; track 22: violin and piano

from 'American' Suite, Op. 98

Antonín Dvořák (1841–1904)
arr. KB & DB

This piece by the great Czech composer Dvořák is the fifth movement of his 'American' Suite (so-called because Dvořák was in New York when he wrote it). It was originally written for piano in 1894 then orchestrated over the following year. In the Suite this movement has no title, but it has many of the features of traditional Czech folk music, which Dvořák often used in his compositions. Contrast the vitality of the opening minor section with the tenderness of the A major section. Omit the repeat of the first section on the D.S.

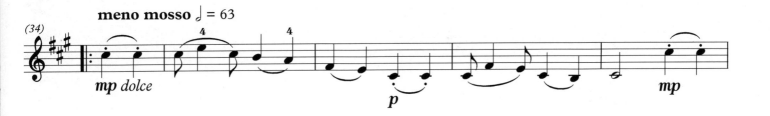

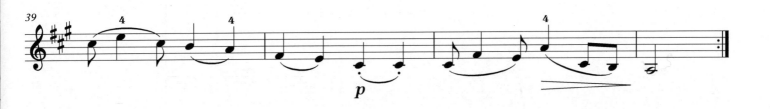

13

10. The crystal spring

track 11

English trad.
arr. KB & DB

This English folksong was collected by Cecil Sharp, the great collector of English folksongs and dances, in Somerset in 1904. The words tell the story of a young sea captain wooing his sweetheart 'down by the crystal spring, where the nightingales sing'.

11. Softly awakes my heart

from *Samson and Delilah*

track 12

Camille Saint-Saëns (1835–1921)
arr. KB & DB

The French composer Saint-Saëns is well known for his popular composition *The Carnival of the Animals*. 'Softly awakes my heart' was originally an aria for mezzo-soprano in his grand opera *Samson and Delilah*, based on the biblical story. The French title, 'Mon cœur s'ouvre à ta voix', literally means 'my heart opens itself to your voice', and the aria is sung by Delilah as she tries to persuade Samson to reveal the secret of his strength. Aim for an expressive performance with legato playing. Thinking about where a singer might breathe will help shape the phrases.

12. Andante

from Piano Sonata in C, K545

Wolfgang Amadeus Mozart (1756–91)

arr. KB & DB

The great Classical composer Mozart wrote numerous symphonies, concertos, and sonatas for both piano and violin. He also wrote many operas, and the melody line in this Andante (the second movement of a piano sonata written in 1788) might suggest an operatic aria sung by a soprano. The left hand of the piano uses the 'Alberti bass'—a characteristic feature of the Classical style. The dynamics are editorial suggestions.

13. Adagio and Allegro

from Sonatina in A for violin and continuo

track 14 (Adagio)

Georg Philipp Telemann (1681–1767)

ed. KB & DB

These are the first two movements of the Sonatina in A for violin and continuo TWV 41:A2 from a set of six by the prolific Baroque composer Telemann. The rapid string-crossing passages and the double stopping at the cadences in the Allegro are characteristic features of Baroque violin music. The dynamics are suggestions only, and the trills should begin on the upper note.

* The bracketed notes may be omitted.

14. La fille aux cheveux de lin

from *Premier livre de préludes*

track 16: piano only;
track 23: violin and piano

Claude Debussy (1862–1918)

arr. KB & DB

La fille aux cheveux de lin	The girl with the flaxen hair	cédez ... (au) mouvt. [mouvement]	rit. ... (a) tempo
très calme et doucement expressif	very calm and sweetly expressive	sans lourdeur	without heaviness
sans rigueur	without rigour	très doux	very sweet
un peu animé	a little livelier	murmuré et en retenant peu à peu	whispering and holding back little by little

This piece is from Debussy's first book of *Préludes* for piano (1910), a set of 12 contrasted pieces depicting different scenes and moods. With its rich harmonies and colours and subtle use of rhythm, Debussy's music evokes atmosphere and mood, and has been seen as the musical equivalent of Impressionism, an artistic movement which aimed to capture an impression of a moment (although Debussy himself was not keen that this label was applied to his music).

for Iain

15. Escape attempt

Kathy and David Blackwell

This piece is in the style of a 'moto perpetuo', a term meaning 'perpetual motion'. Pieces in this style usually consist of a series of rapid even notes and are often very virtuosic, for example Rimsky-Korsakov's *The Flight of the Bumble Bee* or Paganini's *Moto Perpetuo*, Op. 11 (one of the most famous examples for violin). Practise slowly at first to ensure that your right and left hands are well coordinated, then use a metronome to build up the speed. You could start by playing eight quavers to a bar, and then add the semiquavers. The ending should sound mysterious—did the violinist escape?

16. Giga

from Sonata in D minor, Op. 5 No. 7

track 18

Arcangelo Corelli (1653–1713)
ed. KB & DB

This is the final movement of the Sonata in D minor for violin and continuo, Op. 5 No. 7, by the great Italian Baroque violinist and composer Arcangelo Corelli. Corelli's Op. 5 collection is one of the most celebrated sets of violin sonatas ever composed. Dance-like movements were widely used in instrumental sonatas in the seventeenth and eighteenth centuries, and this movement is a jig—a lively dance in 6/8 time. The dynamics in bars 30, 55, 57, and 64 are original; the others are editorial.